WOMEN
GROUNDBREAKERS

WOMEN IN SPORTS

Katie Kawa

PowerKiDS press.

New York

Published in 2016 by The Rosen Publishing Group, Inc.
29 East 21st Street, New York, NY 10010

First Edition

Editor: Sarah Machajewski
Book Design: Reann Nye

Photo Credits: Cover (background) mexrix/Shutterstock.com; cover (Rudolph), p. 9 Mark Kauffman/ The LIFE Picture Collection/Getty Images; cover (Williams sisters) LUIS ACOSTA/AFP/Getty Images; cover (Hamm) Al Messerschmidt/Getty Images Sport/Getty Images; p. 5 Al Tielemans/Sports Illustrated/ Getty Images; p. 6 Scott Halleran/Getty Images Sport/Getty Images; p. 7 New York Daily News Archive/ New York Daily News/Getty Images; p. 11 GARCIA/AFP/Getty Images; p. 13 Bob Martin/ Getty Images Sport/Getty Images; p. 15 MARK RALSTON/AFP/Getty Images; p. 17 Robert Beck/ Sports Illustrated/Getty Images; p. 19 Tom Dulat/Getty Images Sport/Getty Images; p. 20 RacingOne/ ISC Archives/Getty Images; p. 21 Lachlan Cunningham/Getty Images Sport/Getty Images; p. 23 Bloomberg/Bloomberg/Getty Images; p. 25 (softball game) The Washington Post/ The Washington Post/Getty Images; p. 25 (AAGPBL logo) http://commons.wikimedia.org/wiki/File:All-American_Girls_Professional_Baseball_League_logo.svg; p. 27 Jonathan Daniel/Getty Images Sport/ Getty Images; p. 28 Stacy Revere/Getty Images Sport/Getty Images; p. 29 Doug Pensinger/ Getty Images Sport/Getty Images.

Library of Congress Cataloging-in-Publication Data

Kawa, Katie.
 Women in sports / Katie Kawa.
     pages cm. — (Women Groundbreakers)
 Includes webography.
 Includes bibliographical references and index.
 ISBN 978-1-4994-1051-8 (pbk.)
 ISBN 978-1-4994-1083-9 (6 pack)
 ISBN 978-1-4994-1095-2 (library binding)
1. Women athletes—History—Juvenile literature. 2. Women coaches (Athletics)—History—Juvenile literature. 3. Women sportswriters—Juvenile literature. 4. College sports for women—Juvenile literature. 5. Professional sports—Juvenile literature. I. Title.
 GV709.K386 2015
 796.082—dc23
                          2015011498

Manufactured in the United States of America

CPSIA Compliance Information: Batch #WS15PK: For Further Information contact Rosen Publishing, New York, New York at 1-800-237-9932

CONTENTS

FROM OUTSIDERS TO GROUNDBREAKERS

Sports have often been viewed as a man's world. Even today, the phrase "you throw like a girl" is used as an insult. Women were granted voting equality in the United States in 1920, but it took until 1972 for women to be seen as equals in the world of college sports. This happened when a law called Title IX was passed. This law says people can't be kept from joining teams, workplaces, or organizations based on their **gender**.

Despite this law, women are still fighting for equality in professional sports in terms of the money they make and the respect they're given. Groundbreakers in the world of women's sports have worked hard to prove that it's a great thing to throw, run, and play all kind of sports "like a girl."

In 2014, Mo'ne Davis used a 70-mile-per-hour (112.6 km/h) fastball to become the first girl to record a **shutout** in the history of the Little League World Series. She showed everyone that throwing like a girl meant throwing like a winner!

A STAR AT MANY SPORTS

In the early 1900s, professional female athletes were almost **nonexistent**. However, Mildred Ella Didrikson Zaharias, who's most commonly known by her nickname "Babe," became famous during this time for her success at a variety of sports.

At the 1932 Olympic Games in Los Angeles, California, Zaharias won two gold medals and one silver medal in track-and-field events. Zaharias was also skilled at basketball, baseball, swimming, tennis, and many other sports.

Zaharias is perhaps best known as a successful golfer. She took up the game in 1933 and won 82 tournaments in her career. In 1950, Zaharias helped cofound the Ladies Professional Golf Association (LPGA), which has grown into a very important organization in the world of women's professional sports.

Nancy Lopez

Babe Didrikson Zaharias

Babe Didrikson Zaharias's success paved the way for other female professional golfers, such as Nancy Lopez. Lopez joined the LGPA in 1977 and won three major professional golf championships and 48 LGPA tour events in her career. Today, she is considered one of the best players in women's professional golf history.

FROM LEG BRACES TO OLYMPIC GOLD

Wilma Rudolph was the first American woman to win three gold medals in one Olympic Games. In the 1960 Olympic Games in Rome, Italy, Rudolph won gold medals in the 100-meter dash, the 200-meter dash, and the 4 x 100-meter relay. During those Olympic Games, Rudolph set Olympic and world records nearly every time she stepped on the track.

Rudolph's success on the track is even more impressive considering the fact that she had difficulty walking when she was young. As a child growing up in Tennessee, Rudolph became sick with **polio**, which made her unable to use her left leg. When she was six years old, she started wearing leg braces. Three years later, the braces came off, and Rudolph started running. She never looked back.

AMAZING ACHIEVEMENTS

Rudolph used her fame to help achieve **civil rights** for African Americans. She refused to attend **segregated** events after winning her gold medals. In fact, the victory celebration in her hometown of Clarksville, Tennessee, was the town's first desegregated event.

Wilma Rudolph

Wilma Rudolph, who was once unable to walk, went from wearing leg braces to being nicknamed the "world's fastest woman."

A HEPTATHLON HERO

Wilma Rudolph inspired many future female athletes. One of them was Jackie Joyner-Kersee. Many believe Joyner-Kersee is the greatest female athlete of all time because of her success in the Olympic heptathlon. In this event, athletes compete in seven different track-and-field events. They earn points based on their performance in each event.

Joyner-Kersee won back-to-back Olympic gold medals in the heptathlon in 1988 and 1992. In the 1988 Olympic Games, she became the first heptathlete to earn more than 7,000 points. Her 7,291 points in those Olympic Games set a world record that, as of 2015, no one has beaten.

Joyner-Kersee won many Olympic track-and-field medals during her career: three gold medals, one silver, and two bronze. She's still the most decorated female track-and-field Olympian in history.

Jackie Joyner-Kersee was named the "Greatest Female Athlete of the 20th Century" by *Sports Illustrated* magazine.

BILLIE JEAN BREAKS BARRIERS

Tennis is a sport that's featured many groundbreaking female athletes. One of the most important is Billie Jean King. During her career as both a singles and doubles tennis player, King won 39 major championships. However, King may be best known for her work toward equality between men and women in tennis.

Before the 1970s, male tennis players made much more money than female tennis players. However, King fought for equal prize money for women in tennis. In 1973, the U.S. Open became the first major tournament to pay men and women equal prize money.

King also helped create the Women's Tennis Association in 1973 and was its first president. In 1974, she helped start the Women's Sports Foundation to increase opportunities for women in sports.

AMAZING ACHIEVEMENTS

In 1973, King beat Bobby Riggs in a tennis match called the "Battle of the Sexes." King's win helped people see that female athletes—and women in general—deserved more respect than they were being given at that time.

Billie Jean King is a member of the Women's Sports Hall of Fame, the International Tennis Hall of Fame, and the National Women's Hall of Fame.

13

THE WILLIAMS SISTERS

Venus and Serena Williams are two of the most famous tennis players in the world. These sisters changed the way people viewed women's tennis players because of their powerful way of playing the game. Together, they became the faces of women's tennis in the early 21st century.

Serena and Venus often played each other in major tournament finals. From 2002 to 2003, Serena won all four Grand Slam titles in a row, which includes wins at the French Open, U.S. Open, Wimbledon, and Australian Open tournaments. In 2002, the Women's Tennis Association ranked Venus Williams as World No. 1 in singles titles. She was the first African American woman to achieve this ranking. Together, the Williams sisters have changed the face of professional tennis.

AMAZING ACHIEVEMENTS

Long before Venus and Serena Williams took to the court, Althea Gibson became the first African American to win the French Open in 1956.

Serena Williams

Venus Williams

Venus and Serena Williams have three Olympic gold medals in doubles tennis. As of 2015, they have a record total of four Olympic gold medals.

A TEAM EFFORT

As individuals, female athletes have made huge strides in the world of sports. However, teams of female athletes working together have also helped break ground in this male-dominated industry.

Women's soccer has grown in popularity in the United States in recent years. The increased interest in women's soccer is often said to be due to the success of the team that played for the United States in the 1999 World Cup tournament.

The 1999 World Cup team set records for television viewers and crowd size at a women's sporting event, with 90,185 fans in the stands for the final between the United States and China. The game went to a **penalty kick shootout**, which the United States won. That exciting victory put women's soccer in the national spotlight and helped female athletes gain more respect than ever before.

Mia Hamm

The players on the 1999 World Cup team became very famous. Mia Hamm was one of them. She won many awards and honors before she retired from professional soccer in 2004.

AMAZING ABBY

The 1999 World Cup team inspired one girl who has become one of the best soccer players of all time. Growing up in Rochester, New York, Abby Wambach was the youngest of seven children, which she said helped her become the tough soccer player she is today.

In 2013, Wambach broke Hamm's record for international goals, becoming the all-time leading international scorer among both male and female soccer players. She's played as part of the United States Women's National Team (USWNT), and she has two Olympic gold medals. In 2004, she became famous for scoring the gold-medal winning goal against Brazil with a **header** in extra time.

Wambach's success as a star in the National Women's Soccer League has also helped professional women's soccer grow in the United States.

As of May 2015, Abby Wambach has scored 180 goals in international play.

WOMEN IN RACING

Women are playing larger and more important **roles** in the sporting world than ever before. However, there are still some sports that are viewed as a "man's game." One of these sports is auto racing. While women are starting to race in larger numbers, they still have to face drivers and fans who believe they don't belong on the racetrack.

The first woman to try to prove these people wrong was Janet Guthrie, who became the first woman to race in the Indianapolis 500 in 1977. She also drove in the race in 1978 and 1979.

Guthrie's success in the Indianapolis 500 paved the way for Danica Patrick, who became the first woman to lead laps of the race in 2005. Patrick was also the first woman to win an **IndyCar** event in a 2008 race in Japan.

JANET GUTH

Danica Patrick

Janet Guthrie and Danica Patrick both raced as IndyCar and NASCAR drivers. Patrick became the first woman to start NASCAR's famous Dayton 500 race from the pole, or lead, position.

A RECORD-BREAKING COACH

Coaching is another area of sports where women are often seen as outsiders in men's territory. However, female coaches in some sports, especially college basketball, have become famous record breakers. In fact, the first college basketball coach to reach 1,000 career wins was a woman.

Pat Summitt reached this milestone in 2009. By the time she retired in 2012, she had 1,098 career wins. This record made her the winningest coach in the history of college basketball.

Summitt coached at the University of Tennessee, a college she attended and played basketball for in the 1970s. Summitt played for the U.S. women's basketball team and won a silver medal at the 1976 Olympic Games. She later coached this team to its first gold medal in 1984.

AMAZING ACHIEVEMENTS

Summitt was diagnosed with Alzheimer's disease in 2011, which is a sickness that leads to memory loss and harms other important brain functions. She has worked to raise awareness about the disease by writing about it.

Pat Summitt was awarded the Presidential Medal of Freedom, the highest **civilian** honor, in 2012. She received it for being an inspiration both on and off the court.

PLAY BALL!

Sports can be about more than playing the game. They can inspire people during hard times. One of the most famous early professional sports leagues did just this. The All-American Girls Professional Baseball League (AAGPBL) was founded in 1943 to continue professional baseball while male ballplayers were serving in World War II.

The AAGPBL's popularity continued even after the war ended. In the 1948 season, over 900,000 fans attended games—the peak of the league's popularity. Although the AAGPBL only lasted until 1954, it's an important part of the history of American sports. It gave over 600 female athletes a chance to play professional baseball.

In 1992, a movie called *A League of Their Own* put the AAGPBL back in the national spotlight. It taught a new generation of people about these important athletes.

The women of the AAGPBL helped pave the way for the millions of girls who play baseball and softball today.

THE WNBA

The most famous women's professional sports league in the United States today is the Women's National Basketball Association (WNBA). Sheryl Swoopes, one of the most successful players in the history of the league, was the first player to join the league in 1996. The WNBA officially began playing games in 1997.

By the beginning of the 21st century, the WNBA had grown to become the most successful women's professional sports league in American history. Its stars, such as Lisa Leslie and Diana Taurasi, have earned national attention for their talents on the court.

The Houston Comets won the first four WNBA championships. Those teams were led by some of the best players in the league, including Tina Thompson. Thompson is the all-time leading scorer in WNBA history and retired with 7,488 points.

The WNBA began with eight teams but has since grown into a 12-team league.

SUCCESS IN THE WORLD OF SPORTS

Women have been displaying their athletic talents for centuries, whether they were accepted or not. However, that's beginning to change. With the passage of Title IX, female college athletes became viewed as legally equal to male athletes. Now, professional female athletes are fighting for that same equality.

Women are also working hard in other areas of the sports industry, including coaching, **journalism**, and officiating. In April 2015, the National Football League made history when it named Sarah Thomas as its first full-time female official. Thanks to the hard work of these women groundbreakers, girls today are able to grow up believing they can find success in the world of sports.

Sarah Thomas

Pam Oliver

Pam Oliver first became a reporter covering NFL games in 1995. Since then, she's become a well-known figure on the sidelines of many televised professional football games.

TIMELINE OF
WOMEN IN SPORTS

1943 - The AAGPBL is founded.

1950 - The LPGA is founded.

1956 - Althea Gibson becomes first African American to win a Grand Slam tennis title when she wins the French Open.

1960 - Wilma Rudolph becomes the first woman to win three gold medals in one Olympic Games.

1961 - Joan Payson becomes the first woman to buy a professional sports team when she buys the New York Mets baseball team.

1972 - Title IX is signed into law, stating that male and female athletes in U.S. colleges must be treated equally.

1973 - Billie Jean King beats Bobby Riggs in tennis's "Battle of the Sexes." That year, the U.S. Open becomes the first major tennis tournament to give equal prize money to men and women.

1974 - Billie Jean King helps found the Women's Sports Foundation.

1975 - Robin Hermann becomes the first female reporter to enter a professional locker room when she is given access to players following the National Hockey League All-Star Game.

1977 - Janet Guthrie becomes the first woman to race in the Indianapolis 500.

1988 - Jackie Joyner-Kersee sets the record for most points in the Olympic heptathlon, with 7,291.

1997 - The first WNBA game is played.

1999 - The U.S. women's soccer team wins the World Cup, bringing more attention to women's soccer and women's sports in general than perhaps ever before.

2008 - Danica Patrick becomes the first woman to win an IndyCar race.

2009 - Pat Summitt reaches the 1,000-win mark in her college-coaching career, becoming the first male or female coach to do so.

2013 - Abby Wambach becomes the all-time leading scorer among male and female international soccer players.

2015 - Sarah Thomas becomes the first full-time female official in the National Football League.

GLOSSARY

civilian: A person who is not in the military or a member of a police or firefighting force.

civil rights: The rights of citizens to political and social equality.

gender: The state of being male or female.

header: A shot made in soccer when a player uses their head to direct the ball.

IndyCar: A kind of auto racing using cars where the wheels stick out beyond the body of the car.

journalism: The collection, writing, and editing of news for presentation.

nonexistent: Not there.

penalty kick shootout: A way of determining the winner of a soccer game after the normal playing time has ended. It involves a set number of players from each team taking alternating shots at the other team's goalie.

polio: A disease of the nerves and spine that often makes a person unable to move certain body parts.

role: A part played in something.

segregated: Divided by race.

shutout: A baseball game in which a pitcher does not allow the other team to score a run.

INDEX

WEBSITES

Due to the changing nature of Internet links, PowerKids Press has developed an online list of websites related to the subject of this book. This site is updated regularly. Please use this link to access the list: www.powerkidslinks.com/wmng/spor